My True Love Gave to Me

My True Love Gave to Me

TWELVE DAYS
OF CHRISTMAS

Illustrated by
Scott McKowen

On the first day of Christmas,

my true love gave to me

a partridge
in a
pear
tree

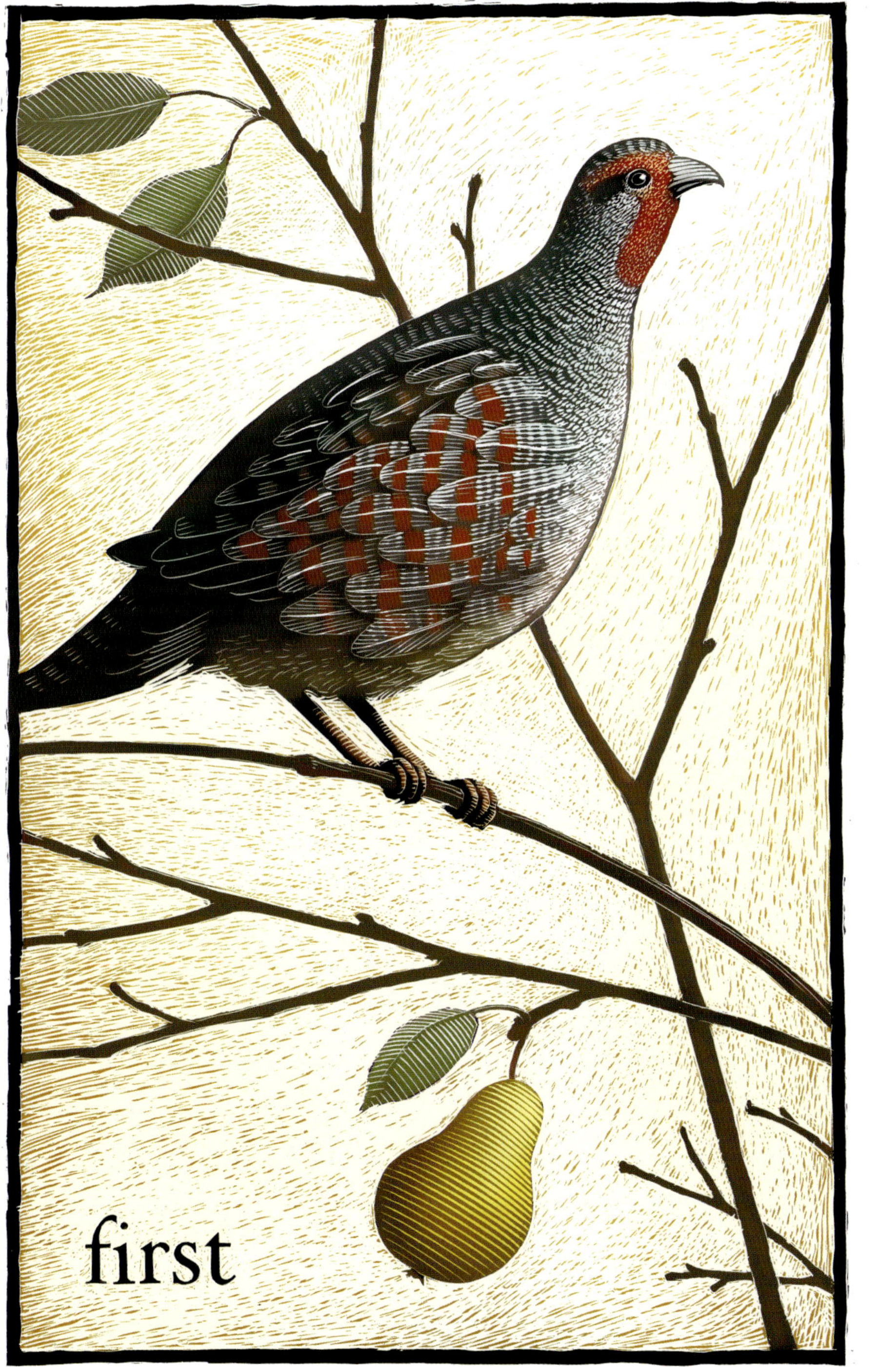
first

On the second day of Christmas,

my true love gave to me

two turtle doves

and a partridge in a pear tree.

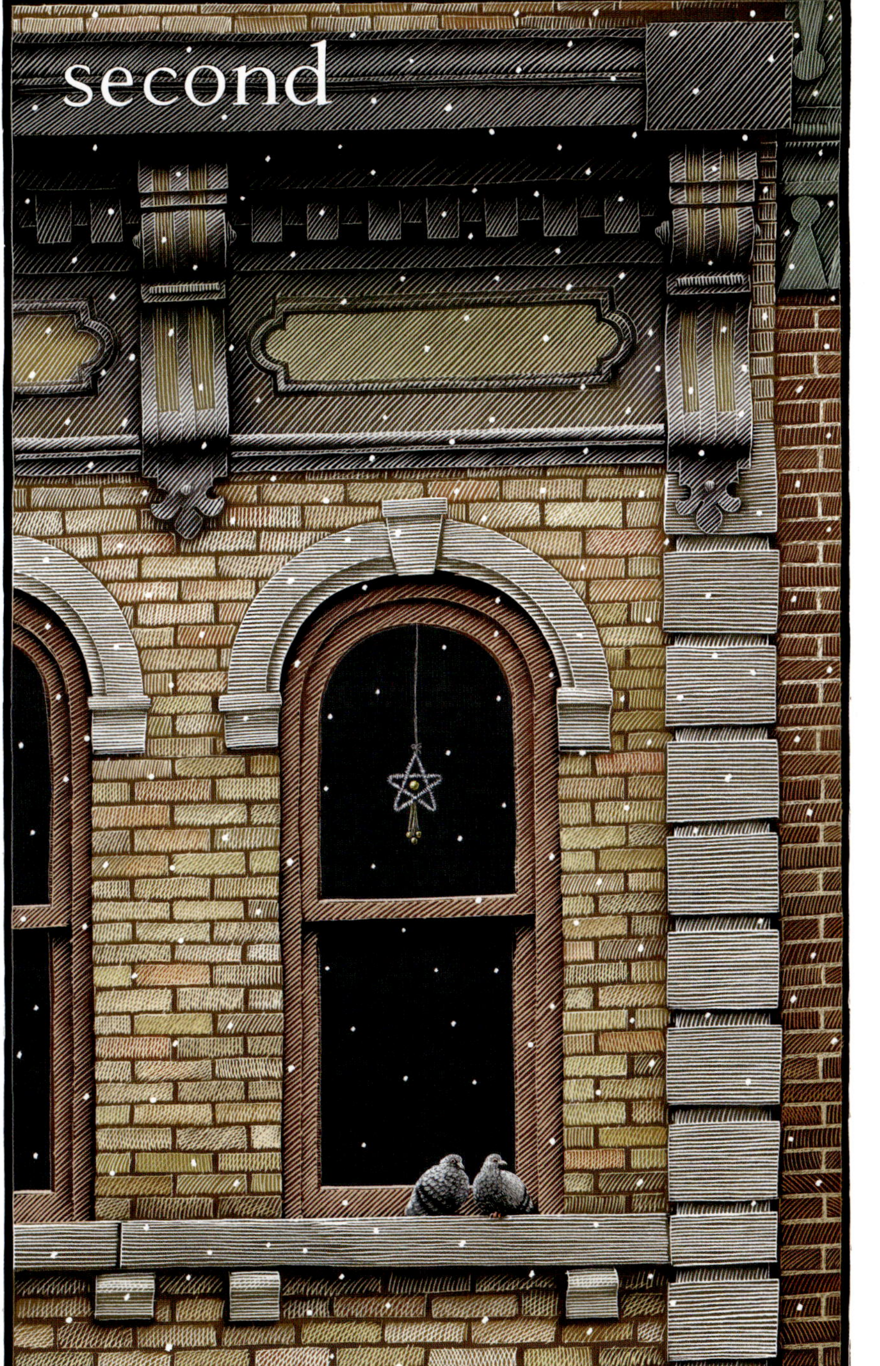
second

On the third day of Christmas,
my true love gave to me

three
french
hens

two turtle doves, and a
partridge in a pear tree.

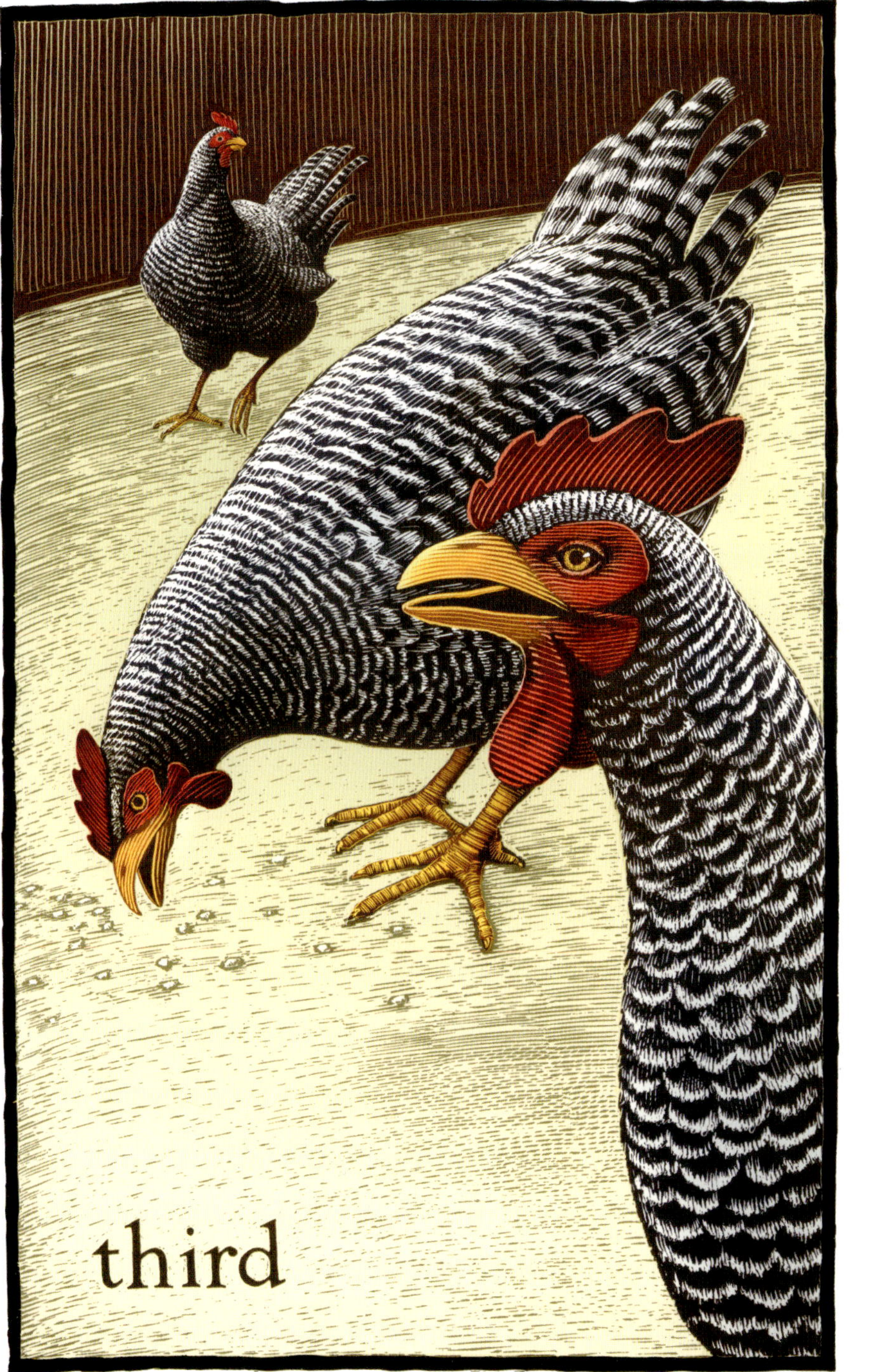
third

On the fourth day of Christmas,
my true love gave to me

four calling birds

three french hens,
two turtle doves, and a
partridge in a pear tree.

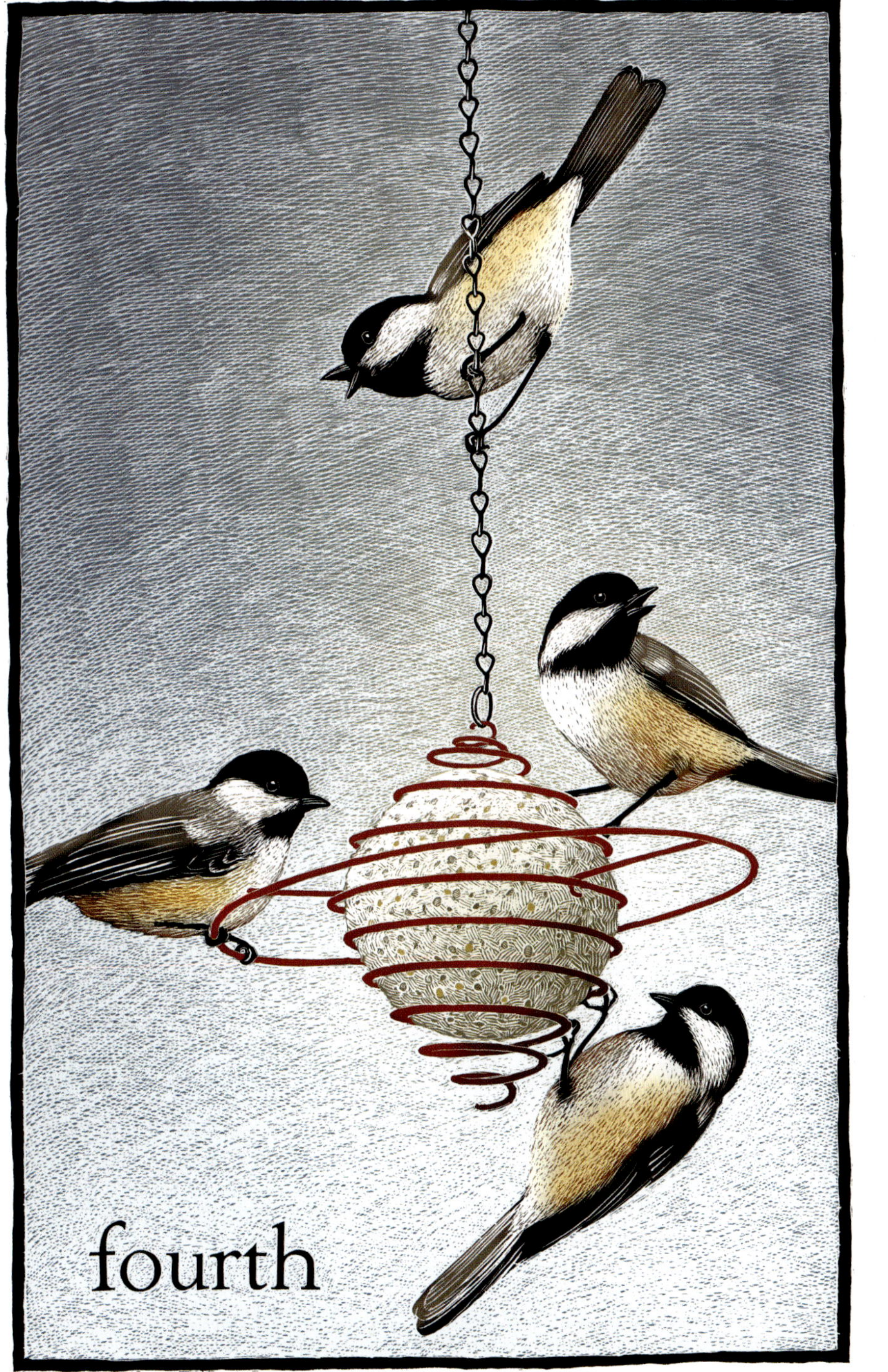
fourth

On the fifth day of Christmas,
my true love gave to me

five gold rings

four calling birds, three french
hens, two turtle doves, and
a partridge in a pear tree.

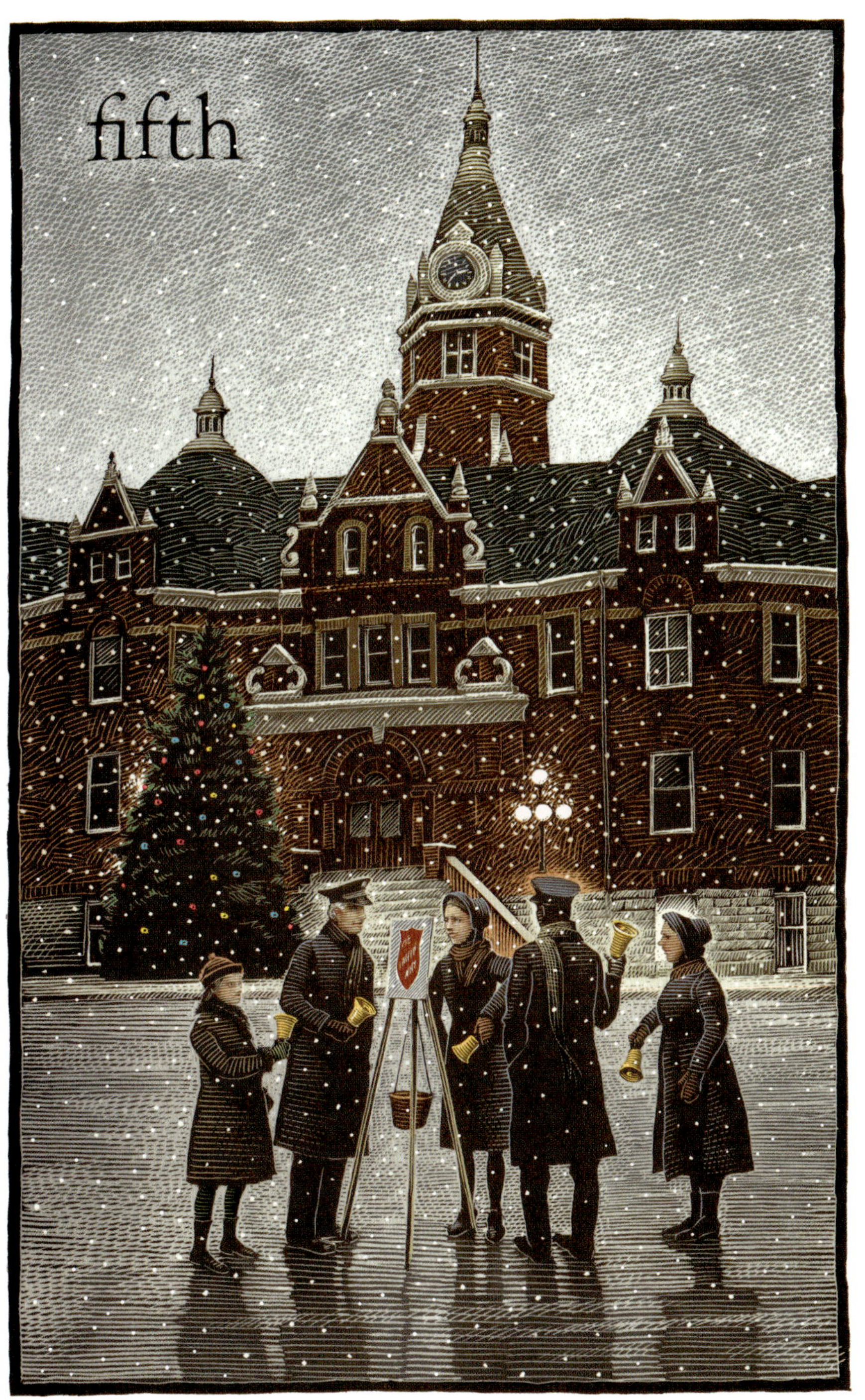
fifth

On the sixth day of Christmas,
my true love gave to me

six geese a-laying

five gold rings; four calling birds,
three french hens, two turtle doves,
and a partridge in a pear tree.

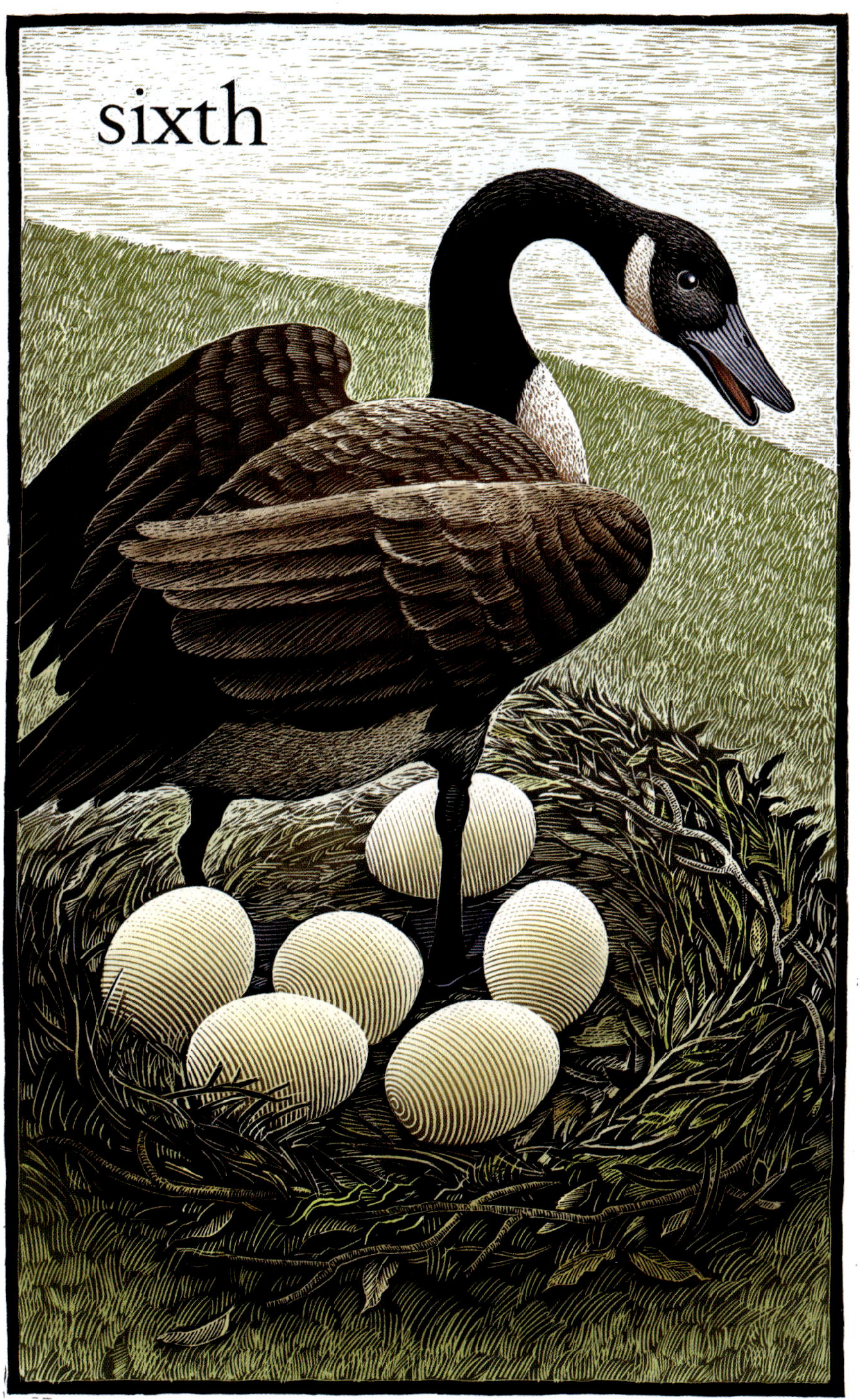
sixth

On the seventh day of Christmas,
my true love gave to me

seven swans a-swimming

six geese a-laying, five gold rings;
four calling birds, three french
hens, two turtle doves, and
a partridge in a pear tree.

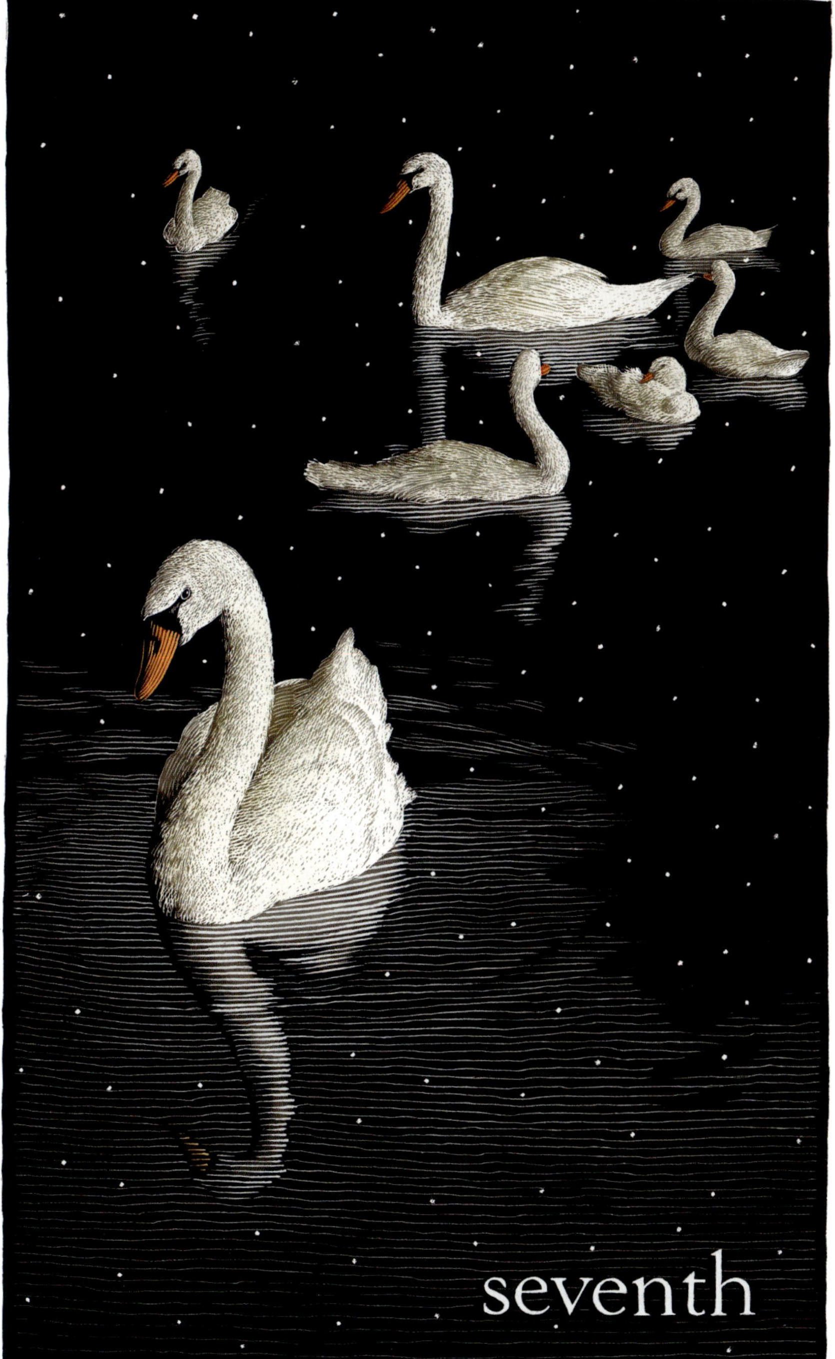
seventh

On the eighth day of Christmas,
my true love gave to me

eight maids a-milking

seven swans a-swimming,
six geese a-laying, five gold rings;
four calling birds, three french
hens, two turtle doves, and
a partridge in a pear tree.

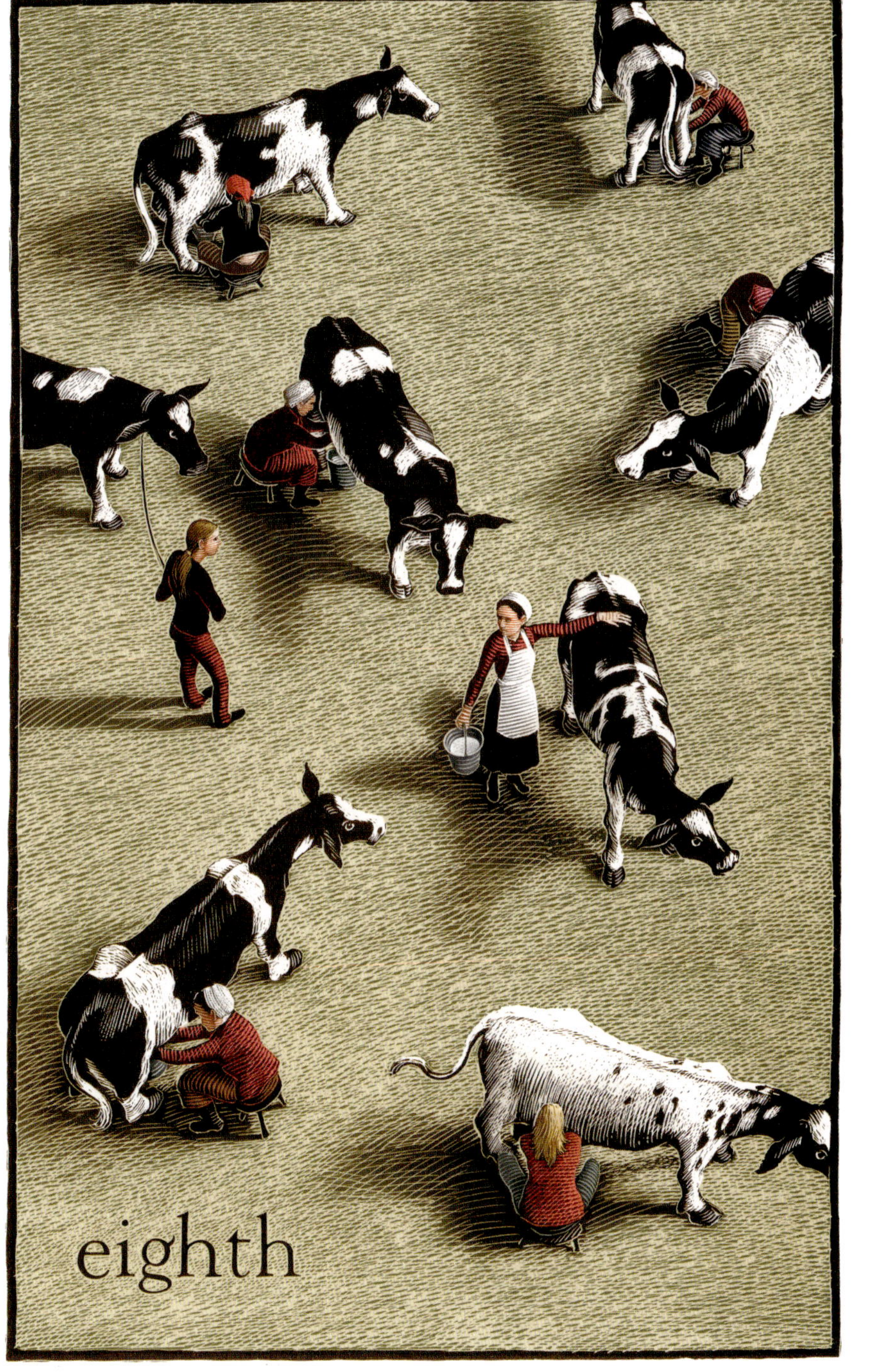
eighth

On the ninth day of Christmas,
my true love gave to me

nine ladies dancing

eight maids a-milking, seven
swans a-swimming, six geese
a-laying, five gold rings; four
calling birds, three french
hens, two turtle doves, and
a partridge in a pear tree.

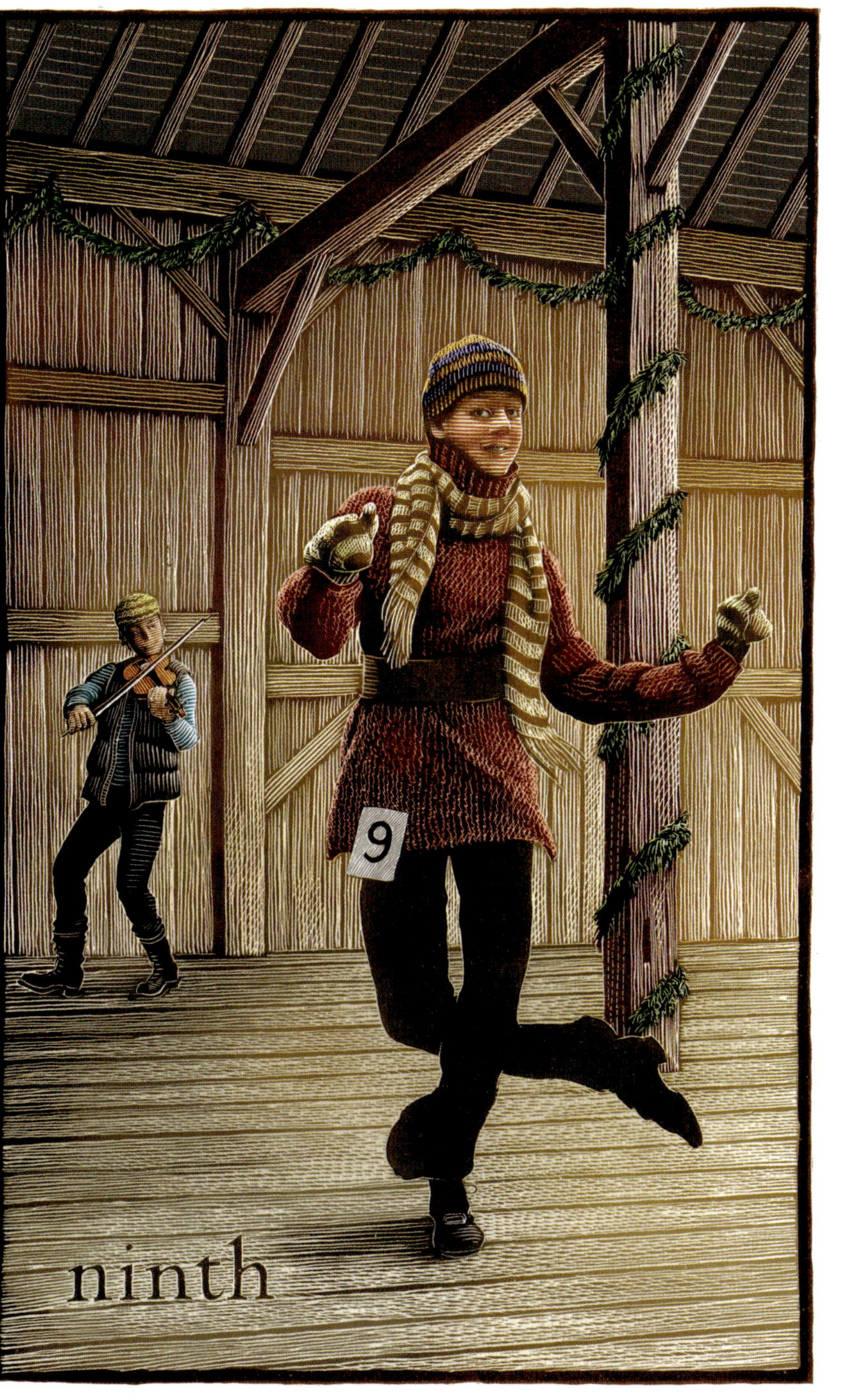
9
ninth

On the tenth day of Christmas,
my true love gave to me

**ten lords
a-leaping**

nine ladies dancing, eight
maids a-milking, seven swans
a-swimming, six geese a-laying,
five gold rings; four calling birds,
three french hens, two turtle doves,
and a partridge in a pear tree.

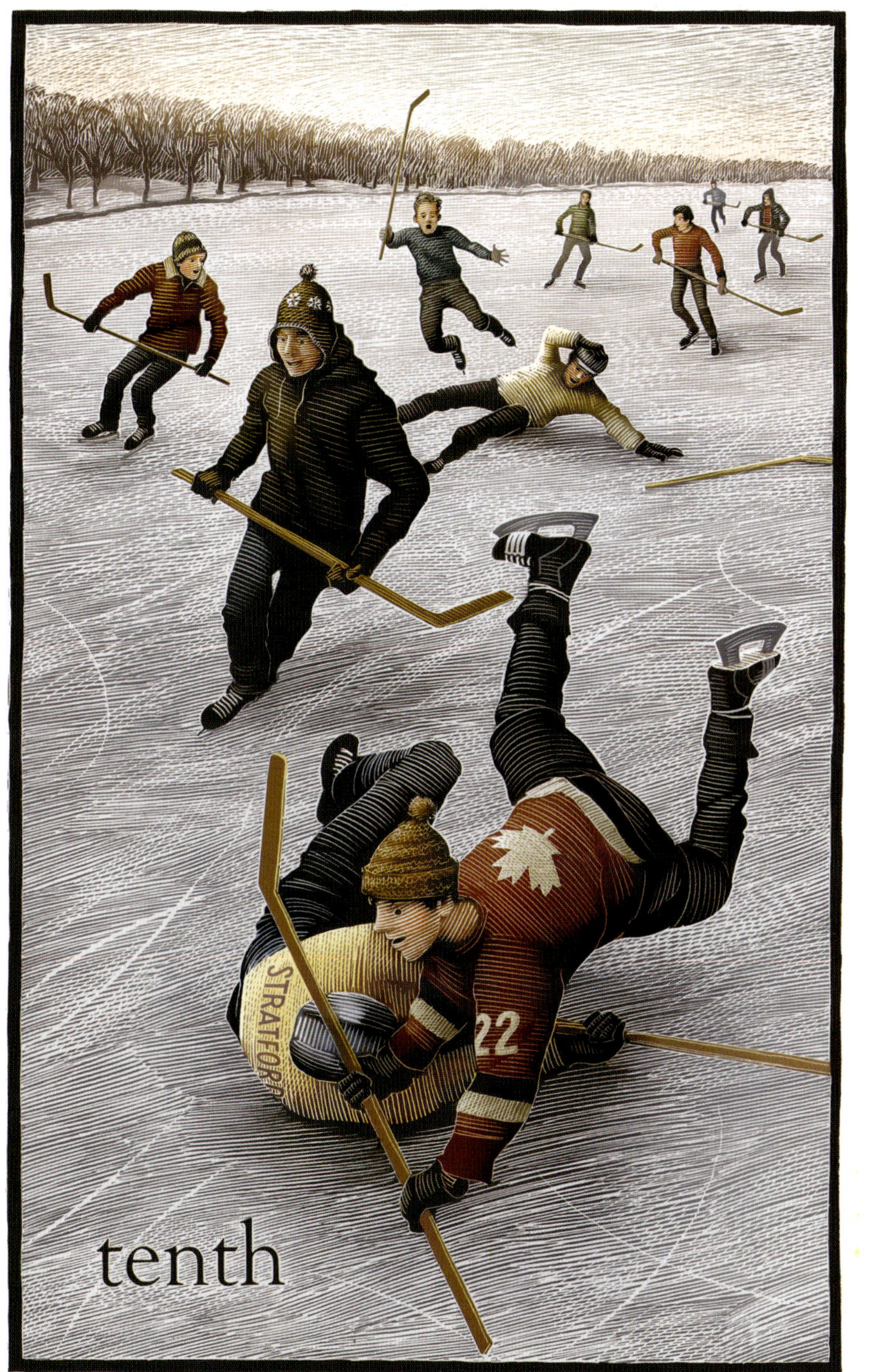

tenth

On the eleventh day of Christmas,
my true love gave to me

eleven
pipers
piping

ten lords a-leaping, nine ladies
dancing, eight maids a-milking,
seven swans a-swimming, six
geese a-laying, five gold rings;
four calling birds, three french
hens, two turtle doves, and
a partridge in a pear tree.

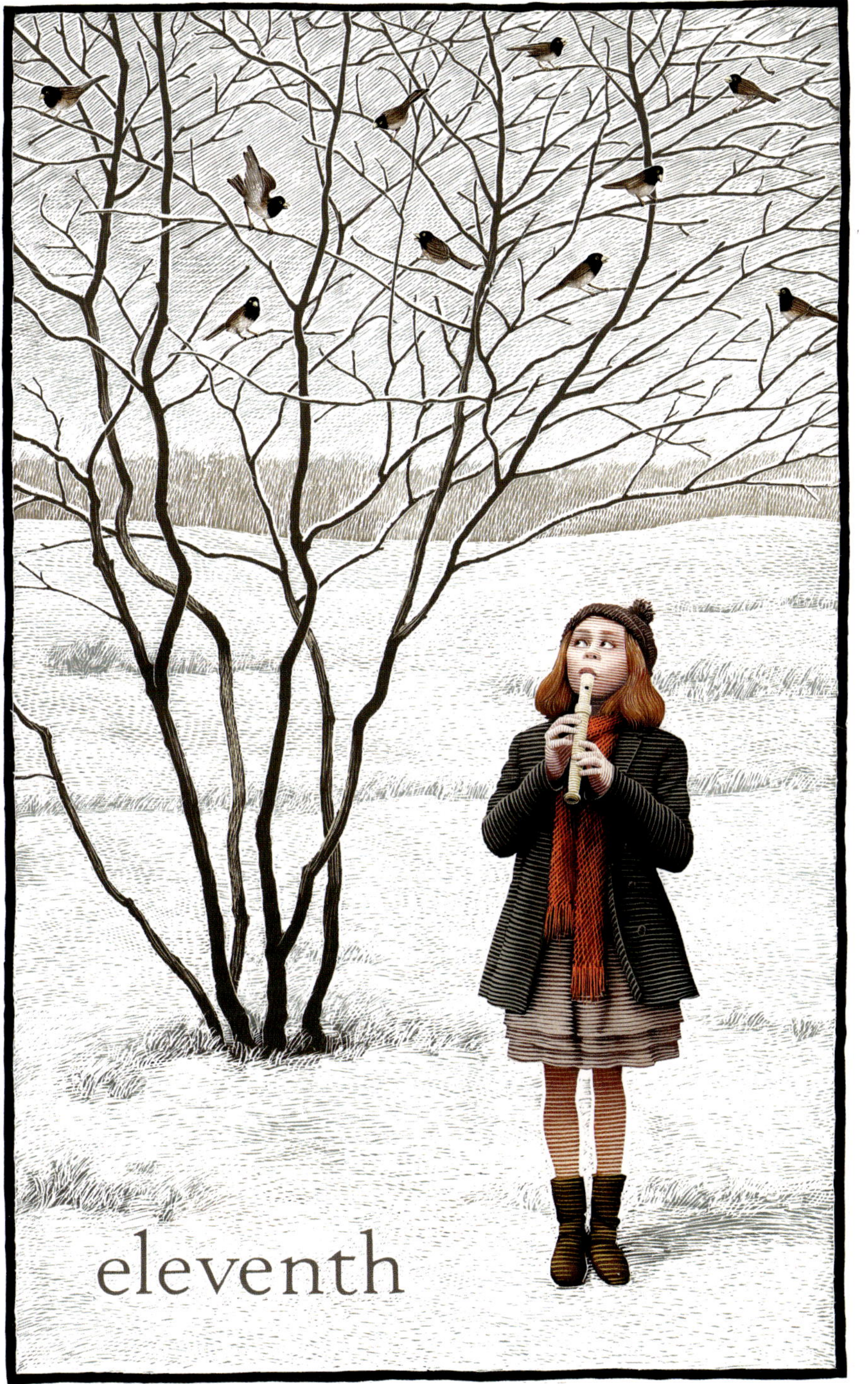

eleventh

On the twelfth day of Christmas,
my true love gave to me

twelve drummers drumming

eleven pipers piping, ten lords
a-leaping, nine ladies dancing,
eight maids a-milking, seven
swans a-swimming, six geese
a-laying, five gold rings; four
calling birds, three french
hens, two turtle doves, and
a partridge in a pear tree.

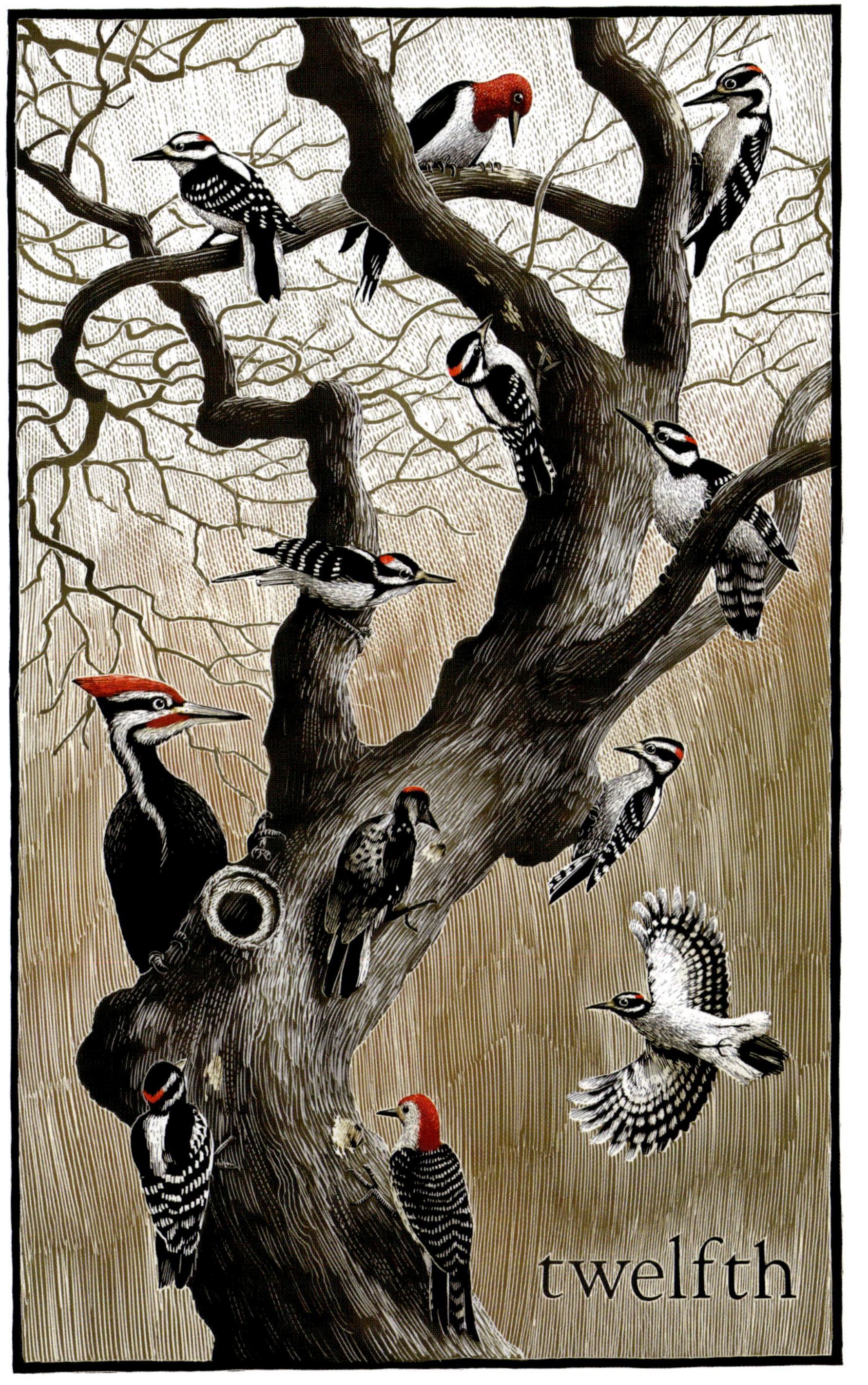
twelfth

TWELVE DAYS IN TWELVE YEARS

I have always designed and printed my own Christmas cards. This enjoyable habit was bred in the bone – my mother created wonderful silkscreened holiday cards every December as far back as the early 1960s. I was her junior apprentice in our improvised basement print shop, and the experience may well have pointed me toward my future career as a graphic designer and illustrator.

My True Love is my wife and creative partner, Christina Poddubiuk. Christina has a busy career as a theater costume and set designer but always manages, between her own deadlines, to find time to collaborate on my illustration projects. We brainstorm together on theater poster concepts or book cover ideas over restaurant dinners and highway drives together. Nobody is keeping score, thank goodness, but the best ideas are almost always hers.

Somehow, holiday cards became part of our shared tradition as well. Every fall, the question "What are we doing for the Christmas card?" would come up. December always seems to be the busiest time of year. Sometimes the card was one more project than we really had time for, so we started experimenting with the idea of a series of cards that would stretch over several years. Starting in 1986, we entertained our friends and ourselves with a fourteen-year series of cards spelling out MERRY CHRISTMAS, one letter each December. We completed that series in 1999, just in time for the turn of the millennium.

In 2000, we started a new series of holiday cards on the theme of The Twelve Days of Christmas – one "day" each year, continuing the format we had established with the alphabet letters. But instead of the traditional Medieval European story-book settings, we wanted to feature the birds, farms and rural traditions in and around our home of Stratford, Ontario, Canada.

We have both Partridges and Pear Trees in our area, so the first illustration was not too much of a stretch. Turtle Doves, however, are a European species – the closest relatives here are mourning doves and, of course, pigeons. Our downtown core retains much of its mid-19th-century architectural character – three-story brick storefronts with handsome cornices. So our Two Turtle Doves became a pair of pigeons (also known as rock doves) huddled together on a window ledge.

We needed to bring our Three French Hens a little closer to home as well. We chose the Barred Rock breed because friends raise them so I had models to work from. I also thought the pattern of their black and white feathers would render beautifully in scratchboard.

We had a suet feeder in our backyard for many years, which was enormously popular with chickadees. They overwinter here so their distinctive song is always in the air – so our Four Calling Birds was an easy and obvious choice.

Five Gold Rings is a curiosity – why is the tune for this verse different from all the others? We didn't want our 2004 card to look like a jewelry store advertisement so we ruled out rings on fingers. Christina was in the middle of designing a production of Bernard Shaw's *Major Barbara* for the Shaw Festival, so the Salvation Army was very much a focus. The problem was solved when we realized that, every December, there are Salvation Army volunteers out collecting donations in front of our City Hall. "Gold Rings" describes the sound of their hand bells.

Canada Geese are widely regarded around the world as a nuisance species – but they are great fun to draw. For compositional reasons I decided to focus on a single large bird on our Six Geese-a-Laying card instead of six small ones – but I gave her six eggs.

Seven Swans a-Swimming was a natural fit because this is the famous civic symbol of our town. Spring doesn't really begin here until the swans are back on the Avon River. There's an annual parade to celebrate "swan weekend." Along with dozens of geese and ducks the swans are released from their winter quarters and waddle down the street to the river, accompanied by a pipe and drum band!

Our town is surrounded by many dairy farms, so Eight Maids a-Milking fit very nicely into the series. The challenge was fitting eight 2000-pound beasts (and eight humans) into a 6" x 9" composition. It occurred to me that an aerial view might be the best way to pull this off. I wondered if I could climb to the top of somebody's silo to get reference photos – but realized that these animals were not exactly going to cooperate with my directions ("you on the far left – turn a little more toward me..."). I found the solution in a change of scale: our local farm co-op store sells beautifully crafted miniature animal figures made by the German company Schleich. The proportions and detail are stunning – I purchased a small Holstein herd and set up the entire composition on the kitchen table.

Dancing was a different kind of challenge – which of the endless range of styles of the art form should we pick for our Nine Ladies? We wanted to focus the series on old rural traditions, so we decided on step dancing – reels, jigs and clogs featuring intricate footwork, accompanied by wonderfully energetic fiddle music. We made inquiries with a local teacher, who recommended a star student to be the model. We met fourteen-year-old Chelsea Mott, and she performed a rousing step dance routine in our front hall while I made reference photos to draw from. (Her dad thoughtfully provided a sheet of Masonite to protect our hardwood floors.) We imagined our scene taking place in a great barn decorated for the holidays.

Ten Lords a-Leaping became a pick-up hockey game on our frozen Avon River. The sense of nostalgia – this is how many hockey fans came to love the game – made this card one of the most popular of the series.

Perhaps it was assumed that our Eleven Pipers Piping would be bagpipers – I had started pencil sketches in that direction – but we thought this was maybe too obvious, and wanted to give it a twist. We decided to simplify, and asked eleven-year-old Effie Honeywell to serenade a flock of juncos, another bird species that overwinters here, with her recorder.

Having come full circle back to birds, we decided that our Twelve Drummers Drumming should be woodpeckers – Hairy, Downy, Red-headed, Red-breasted, and Pileated – all native species that we regularly encounter on our bird watching walks in the woods.

We completed the Twelve Days series in 2012. Luckily for us, Firefly Books has long been on our Christmas card list. Lionel Koffler and Michael Worek had received the cards one by one, and they suggested turning the series into a book – a gift indeed, for us. Christina and I are most grateful to share the project with a wider audience.

SCOTT McKOWEN

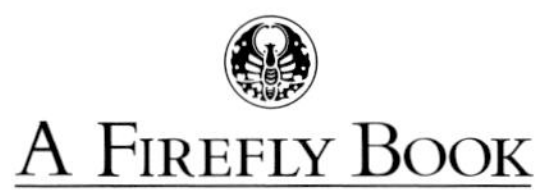

Published by Firefly Books Ltd. 2013

First printing

Publisher Cataloging-in-Publication Data (U.S.)
A CIP record of this title is available from the Library of Congress

Library and Archives Canada Cataloguing in Publication
Twelve days of Christmas (English folk song)
My true love gave to me : twelve days of Christmas /
[illustrated by] Scott McKowen.
ISBN 978-1-77085-231-0
1. Folk songs, English--Texts. 2. Christmas music--Texts. I. McKowen, Scott II. Title. III. Title: Twelve days of Christmas (English folk song).
PZ8.3.T9 2013 782.42'17230268 C2013-901243-5

Published in the United States by Firefly Books (U.S.) Inc.
P.O. Box 1338, Ellicott Station, Buffalo, New York 14205

Published in Canada by Firefly Books Ltd.
50 Staples Avenue, Unit 1, Richmond Hill, Ontario L4B 0A7

Cover and interior design by Scott McKowen
www.punchandjudy.ca
Typeset in Cassia Extra Light.

Printed in China.